CHINESE MOTIFS OF GOOD FORTUNE

Discovering China

CHINESE MOTIFS OF GOOD FORTUNE

Photographs by Liu Shenghui
Text by Zhu Wen

Better Link Press

This book is edited and designed by the Editorial Committee of *Cultural China* series

Managing Directors: Wang Youbu, Xu Naiqing
Editorial Director: Wu Ying
Editors: Yang Xiaohe, Kirstin Mattson
Editorial Assistant: Xu Xinyan

Photographs by Liu Shenghui
Text by Zhu Wen
Translation by Cao Jianxin

Cover and Interior Design: Yuan Jielin

ISBN: 978-1-60220-119-4

Address any comments about *Discovering China: Chinese Motifs of Good Fortune* to:

Better Link Press
99 Park Ave
New York, NY 10016
USA

or

Shanghai Press and Publishing Development Company
F 7 Donghu Road, Shanghai, China (200031)
Email: comments_betterlinkpress@hotmail.com

Printed in China by Shenzhen Donnelley Printing Co. Ltd.

1 2 3 4 5 6 7 8 9 10

Contents

Preface

What do we mean by auspicious symbols? And why have they been so important in China throughout the ages, appearing on works of art, porcelains, furniture, architectural decoration and so many other places?

The following chapters thoroughly discuss the different types and connotations of auspicious symbols, whether they be animals, plants, figures, objects or abstract patterns. First, however, we will take a look at the history and enduring popularity of using symbols to invoke wishes for good fortune, in its many forms.

One of the oldest classical Chinese texts, the *I Ching* or *Book of Changes*, discusses methods for predicting and shaping the future. It defines auspice as "the state of being free from any unfavorable influence," which is universally understood to means luckiness and fortune. Then what does "fortune" mean? Different people may have different answers to this question. Some regard peace and safety as fortune while others would define fortune as having good health. For some, fortune may be represented by large number of descendants, while others deem it fortunate to possess wealth.

While fortune has a multi-layered meaning, at its core, it has remained essentially unchanged for hundreds of years. Lying at its heart are the traditional "Five Fortunes" expounded in another important ancient Chinese text, the *Shang Shu* or *Collection of Ancient Texts*: longevity, affluence, good health, virtue and "natural death." That is to say, if one remains healthy and peaceful both physically and psychologically, behaves virtuously and benevolently, possesses a considerable amount of wealth, lives for a long time, and eventually dies without any pain, conflict or worry, then he or she is fortunate in its truest and most comprehensive sense.

Over five thousand years, the pursuit of fortune has made its mark on the culture and even the psychology of China. Traditionally, the Chinese hold "benevolence" as their highest moral standard, believing that all fortune stems from virtue. Opposing wars and aggression, seeking a peaceful and prosperous world, and taking pleasure in living a simple and carefree life are, therefore, priorities. The pursuit of "fortune," whether consciously or subconsciously, means treating every living thing more kindly and mercifully, sharing good wishes and creating a peaceful and happy environment.

Foretelling fortune through divination and astronomical observation has been important since ancient times. These activities have been seen as a way to attain benefits and avoid disasters. However, pursuing fortune extends beyond purely mystical or spiritual activities into many facets of life in China, as people routinely say lucky words, use auspicious patterns, and carry out various activities to invoke fortune.

To categorize, there are auspicious articles (e.g. various types of statues), auspicious activities (e.g. traditional festivals), and auspicious behaviors (e.g. divination and prayer). In terms of forms of expression, there is spoken language (e.g. auspicious statements), written characters (e.g. supplicatory and laudatory passages), visual representations (e.g. auspicious pictures and patterns), tangible utensils (e.g. magical tools for dispelling evil) and so on.

Among these categories, pictures and patterns with desirable allegorical connotations can be seen most often and are applied the most extensively. For thousands of years, these auspicious pictures and patterns have been incorporated into daily life through various artistic techniques. They are so prevalent that it can be said that "every picture is sure to have an auspicious connotation." These meanings can come about because of a relation to a myth or legend, or they can be due to the intrinsic qualities of the object that is depicted. Because many words in spoken Chinese are homophones, i.e. they have different meanings but sound the same, the picture's symbolism may be due to a homophonous connotation.

Auspicious symbols are prevalent in design and decoration, serving to eliminate negatives while invoking fortune. They appear at every stratum of society, as well as in every media: architecture, sculpture, painting, textiles, metal and pottery, among others. Over centuries, a myriad of beautiful patterns and shapes have been created to help build an auspicious environment. Different symbols may serve to express good wishes, invoke wealth or health, and eliminate evil or give warning. The symbols often have deep links to aspects of traditional Chinese culture, relating to Taoism, Confucianism and Buddhism and well as feudal history.

In the following chapters, we will look at traditional auspicious patterns classified into those featuring animals, plants, figures, objects and symbols, as well as those that combine patterns from different categories. Using these categories, this book will introduce common patterns, discussing their history, meaning and use.

Bats, peaches, mythological immortals, incense burners, Chinese characters—these are just a small sampling of the images that appear in the decorative arts of China. The images can be admired for their beauty alone, but learning their meanings brings another level of appreciation. Let's together step into this intricate world of symbolism, so as to begin to understand this vivid aspect of Chinese culture that surrounds us when walking through buildings, gazing at art, using furniture, or collecting textiles and porcelains. In fact, once you learn this "visual language," these symbols will appear in unexpected corners and details, providing a fascinating glimpse of the profound traditional culture of China.

A gourd-shaped decoration on the screen implies fortune and prosperity because the word for gourd is homophonous with a word for good fortune (福禄) in Chinese.

Chapter One   Animals

Among the many auspicious symbols, those with animals as their subject can be seen most often, perhaps due to the fact that animal worship can be traced very far back in human history. The animals pictured include both the real and the imaginary. From mythologies and legends, there are various types of evil-dispelling auspicious creatures, while from real life, there are rare and exotic birds and beasts, as well as domestic animals. The allegorical connotations of these animals can relate to luck, longevity, wealth, accomplishment and destiny. Some animals may have more than one auspicious connotation.

Various types of traditional patterns or decorations spring from ancient mythologies and legends. Images of divine animals include the dragon, phoenix, kylin (which has the body of a deer, tail of a cow, a horn on its head, and scales all over the body), *bixie* (a legendary evil-dispelling creature resembling a winged lion), *Canglong* (Grey Dragon, Eastern God in Chinese mythology), *Baihu* (White Tiger, Western God in Chinese mythology), *Zhuque* (Vermillion

The Chinese dragon is a divine animal with many associations, such as good fortune, harmony and prosperity, which makes it quite different from the dragon known through Western legends. Representing supreme status, the Chinese dragon is extensively applied in various designs for buildings, furniture and household items. For example, the suspension hook of this birdcage is in the shape a dragon. A common Chinese phase, "as strong and vigorous as a wandering dragon," applies here, with the sinuous and soaring design in a perfect combination with the practical requirement of the suspension hook. In spite of its small size, it shows exquisite workmanship, with the entire dragon, including its head, claws, and even the scales on its body, engraved in a lifelike way. The dragon theme has also been extended into other structures of this birdcage, integrating and perfecting the entire work.

Bird, Southern God in Chinese mythology) and *Xuanwu* (Black Warrior, Northern God in Chinese mythology), which combines a tortoise and snake.

As divine animals in the heavenly palace as well as patrons of mortals, these creatures speed across the sky on clouds and mists with an amazing magic power. Symbolic of good fortune and festivity, they represent general aspirations for a lofty and venerable status, while some specifically serve to protect domiciles and attract luck. Therefore, their images were often applied in the decorations of both royal buildings as well as articles for daily use. For example, a flying dragon might be found twine around a *huabiao*, an ornamental column erected in front of a palace or tomb; the bronze image of a kylin in front of a palace; and dragons and phoenixes embroidered onto imperial bed curtains and quilts.

Real-life birds and animals that have auspicious connotations include the lion, tiger, crane, deer, bat and magpie. Some of them can chase away evil with their strength, courage and ferocity. For example, the stone lions often seen in front of the gate of a house serve as protectors. Some animals may invoke wishes for good fortune because of their names—e.g. the magpie symbolizing

The top of this whitewashed wall is decorated with a large black dragon. We can see clearly that the shape of dragon actually blends the parts of many animals: the buckhorn, representing longevity; the cow-ear, connoting the highest status; the tiger-eye, denoting majesty; the lion-nose, symbolizing prosperity and honor; and the horse-teeth, symbolizing diligence and kindness. In addition, it has a snake-neck, fish-scales and hawk-claws. The legendary dragon's composite structure signifies that it is the head of all animals as well as an omnipotent god. This uniquely-shaped decoration is a highlight of the garden, and enriches its atmosphere of prosperity, good fortune and nobility.

luckiness, and bat connoting bliss—due to the fact that these words are homophones in Chinese.

Domestic birds and beasts with which human beings have had a longstanding relationship—the horse, sheep, chicken, cattle and fish—are partners that people cannot live without. People not only benefit from them, but also feel deeply grateful to them, and therefore, they have assumed many fortunate connotations. The names of some of these animals were even homophonous with auspicious words in the ancient Chinese language; for example, "sheep" is homophonous with "auspicious," while "chicken" is homophonous with "lucky." And, since "fish" is homophonous with "surplus," fish often serve as the subject for pictures for Spring Festival (the beginning of the Lunar New Year), invoking the wish for plentitude in the new year.

Different animals are often pictured together, combining to represent a new symbol or reinforce the original meaning. Some frequent combinations include the dragon and phoenix together, which can represent wishes for a happy marriage and fulfilling life, and the tortoise and crane together, symbolizing longevity.

Domestic residences in the Chinese style often feature a simple combination of whitewashed wall and black tiles. However, the seemingly simple pattern can be enhanced by many symbolic connotations. Here, the engraved tile decoration on the gable wall is a traditional pattern called "a dragon frolicking with a pearl," demonstrating cheerfulness. The "ridge-swallowing beast" atop the house is, according to the legend, one of the nine sons of the dragon. In Buddhist scripture, it is under the throne of the God of Rain, giving *chiwen* the power to extinguish fire, so it is often ensconced on both ends of the ridge of a house, serving to protect against disasters and fires. The large patch of whitewashed wall sets off these exquisite tile-engravings, much like the play of white paper against black ink in traditional Chinese paintings, bringing a luxurious feeling to the simple coloring.

In this picture, we can see on the ridge of a house the image of *chiwen*, one of the legendary nine sons of the dragon. With a dragon-head and fish-body, and its tail sticking high up, *chiwen* opens its mouth as if about to swallow the ridge. This so-called "ridge-swallowing beast" invokes protection for the house and chases away anything evil.

There are two different double dragon patterns in this picture. The stone-engraved dragon pattern on the upper wall is circular, with the upper dragon being a "descending dragon," and the lower one an "ascending dragon." In contrast, the pattern on the handle of the wood-decorated door below is rectangular, with two dragons symmetrically mounted left and right, in a posture of a "running dragon." On the upper stone panel, the dragons have been engraved realistically, with a vivid and lifelike posture, while the two dragons on the door handle have been abstracted, symbolically invoking the majesty of the dragon. These two contrasting double dragon patterns not only highlight the decorative effect of the space, but shed light on the variety possible within one type of Chinese auspicious pattern.

According to legend, the nine sons of the dragon display different capabilities and characteristics. This classically-shaped door-knocker represents *jiaotu*, the sixth son of dragon. Resembling a conch or clam, *jiaotu* is a lover of a solitary life, hating to see others enter its den. As a conch or clam closes its shell against the invasion of any foreign object, people adopt its image on their doors and gates, invoking its ability to close itself to provide protection. In addition, according to a legend, it can keep away any base and mean person, serve as a protector for child-bearing, and secure academic success and promotion in government. The wood engraving above the door-knocker features a legendary story as its subject, which together with the picture of *jiaotu*, gives the door a strong classical appeal.

While big red lanterns in and of themselves are typically associated with China, this lantern's decoration has even more abundant Chinese characteristics, including its hexagonal shape and decorations of wood-engraved flying dragons. These dragons, which feature a realistic head together with an abstracted body, demonstrate the variety of decorative technique, while the realism used in representing the head reinforce its meanings of "chief" and "outstanding." The number of dragons coincides with the auspicious saying, "The number six symbolizes success and smoothness." Although the lantern is small, it contains a desirable allegorical meaning throughout, from color to shape.

A classical style in traditional Chinese furniture is Ming-dynasty furniture, famous around the world for its simple lines and its upright and elegant shapes. This "southern yoke-backed armchair" reflects the refined Ming-dynasty style, and is decorated only on the seat back. A careful look reveals that the pattern of decoration is a dragon roundel, with its head located in the center, and its body and feet abstracted into many curves winding around it. The abstract dragon pattern, like other dragon images, symbolizes a wish for status and fortune.

Detail of the dragon roundel pattern

This piece of furniture served as a washstand in ancient China. Even such a practical piece of furniture has exquisite details—two dragons as the decoration on its top, with their heads carved meticulously and vividly, project a majestic air. Openwork cloud-patterns with smooth lines have been applied below the dragons, giving the feeling that they are speeding across the sky on clouds. With fluid lines and refined detail, this furniture, echoing with the adjacent ornamental perforated window, embodies the traditional pursuit of exquisiteness and perfection in design.

Detail of the dragon-head on the washstand

In traditional Chinese buildings, a screen is often attached beneath the beam between columns, and is usually used for spatial partition and interior decoration. As the screen in this picture does not touch the floor, it is called an "overhanging screen." While this wood-engraved overhanging screen has the dragon as its basic pattern, it combines the dragon with the phoenix to enhance its symbolic meaning. While the dragon is the head of all animals in Chinese mythology, the phoenix is the king of all birds. Picturing these two divine animals together traditionally indicates prosperity, invoking a dignified and respectable status. Although the phoenix can be either male or female, when placed next to a mighty and majestic dragon, it usually plays the role of a beautiful female. Therefore, the dragon and the phoenix often figuratively represent a male and female with an elevated status. This picture also can represent a wish for a happy marriage or fulfilling life.

This picture shows a detail of an elongated bridle joint stone that is part of the memorial archway in the Ancestral Temple in Foshan, Guangdong Province. This type of stone is typical of memorial archways, and the one shown here features exquisite engraving, with a phoenix soaring over the clouds and looking back at the fiery sun in the distant horizon. The phoenix of ancient legend would fly to a peaceful and prosperous place, making it a divine and auspicious bird. In addition, just like the dragon, the phoenix symbolized imperial power in ancient China, as well as the spirit of the Chinese people. Therefore, this stone engraved pattern connotes festivity and fortune, and its composition also perfectly compliments the shape of the joint stone. While small, this elongated bridle joint stone is refined and magnificent, representing the perfect finishing touch to the entire archway.

Although the furniture and fittings are not classical, this spacious room does feature a roof-truss typical of ancient Chinese buildings. Each of the wood beams of the roof-truss is engraved with an exquisite pattern of the phoenix and auspicious cloud. A divine bird, the Chinese phoenix embodies such qualities as morality, good fortune, cleanliness, beauty, love and kingship. The auspicious cloud also represents a desirable destiny because "cloud" is homophonous with "luckiness." Therefore, the pattern consisting of a phoenix and auspicious cloud invokes a wish for luck and fortune.

This piece of furniture is made up of three sections—a front and rear screen with a clothes-rack in the middle. While the clothes-rack features a golden phoenix in the center, the screens are decorated on the corners with golden engravings of the "Four Divine Animals." In ancient China, people divided the sky into eastern, western, southern and northern sections, naming each section after its shape, formed by linking seven major constellations within the section. The eastern section was named for *Canglong* (Grey Dragon), the western section for *Baihu* (White Tiger), the southern section for the *Zhuque* (Vermillion Bird) and the northern section for the *Xuanwu* (Black Warrior). In ancient legends, these gods guarding the sky were divine animals with magic powers that could frighten away demons and evils. There is an old saying in China, "A dragon on the left and a tiger on the right can dispel all misfortunes, while *Zhuque* and *Xuanwu* can bring harmony." Therefore, since ancient times, people have expressed their wishes to chase away evil and achieve happiness through images of these animals. Here, the designer has created a striking work of art that contrasts elements of traditional Chinese culture with simple, modern shapes.

Just like calligraphy, painting and poetry, seal-carving is one of the four traditional Chinese arts, and as such, it embodies and represents Chinese culture. In this picture, a piano has been skillfully placed within a space encircled by four huge seals. The tops of the seals are each engraved with one of the Four Divine Animals—*Canglong, Baihu, Zhuque* and *Xuanwu*—thus not only reflecting tradition but also evoking wishes to dispel evil and invite good fortune. In the images below, we can see the details of them. As the Northern God, the *Xuanwu*, which combines the tortoise and snake, is also regarded as the God of Water, because it lives in rivers, lakes and seas. Since longevity is associated with the tortoise, the *Xuanwu* has also become a symbol of immortality.

Detail of the *Xuanwu* (Black Warrior, left) and *Canglong* (Grey Dragon, right)

Detail of the *Baihu* (White Tiger)

Detail of the *Zhuque (Vermillion Bird)*

This is a vermilion lacquer kylin engraved in wood. An auspicious animal in ancient legends, the kylin has the body of a deer and tail of a cow, and has a horn on its head, as well as scales all over its body. Like the phoenix, the kylin can be male or female. A beast for gods to ride, the kylin is also a benevolent animal, and a symbol of peace and longevity. Since it has flesh growing on the end of its horns, the kylin is known as "an animal that does no harm to people even though it has a weapon." The kylin is also believed to bring success in providing descendants. People often express their wish for fortune and fruitfulness by placing such a decoration in their homes. Since the kylin integrates the images of many animals, it embodies the traditional Chinese ideology of "integrating all beauties." There are many wonderful folk legends about the kylin. According to legend, the kylin is a gentle and

amicable animal that does not eat any living insects or break any living grass, conforming to Confucian thought and traditional ethical codes. Another popular legend is that the emergence of the kylin denotes the peace of the world. It is easy to see why the kylin, endowed with so many wonderful qualities, is regarded as a rare and strong auspice. Its display represents a wish for peace, fortune and serenity.

With its raised head, strong chest and penetrating glance, this bronze statue of the kylin, displayed at the Ancestral Temple in Foshan, Guangdong Province, conveys its intrepid and valorous qualities.

This bronze-statue represents a *bixie*, known for its evil-dispelling qualities. A supernatural auspicious animal from legend, the *bixie* resembles a winged lion, capable of eliminating evil, and resisting demons and monsters. In addition, according to legend in southern China, the *bixie* loves to eat valuables such as gold and silver, absorbing treasures from all directions. Since it is seen to be helpful in acquiring fortune, businesspeople like the *bixie* very much, and many people like to put a *bixie* on their table, or carry it with them. According to legend, it is lazy by nature and it enjoys sleep. Therefore, its collectors are advised to play with it every day, so as to awaken it, because only in this way can wealth come to them. This is reflected in the common saying, "Once you touch a *bixie*, you will have good luck; if you touch it again, wealth will come to you continuously; if you touch it for the third time, you will get promoted easily."

Regarded as a tribute in the Han dynasty (206BC – 220AD), the lion has for centuries been seen by the Chinese as an auspicious animal. As it is ferocious and majestic, people often use lion statues to dispel evil and repel ghosts. The lion has also come to be seen as a symbol of authority. The traditional Chinese folk custom that has spread most extensively into foreign countries is none other than the festive dance of the dragon and lion. In the dance, the artistically-rendered lions make lively motions up and down in pursuit of an embroidered ball, expressing the yearning of people for peace and serenity. As the lion-dance is usually the first program in a celebration, the saying "a lion dances with an embroidered ball" is followed by noting that something good is to come. The stone statue seen here used as indoor decoration, takes this as its theme. We first see the lively lion, and then beyond it, we can see the room inside, offering enchanting scenery.

In ancient China, the luxurious house of a noble family would always have pair of stone lions in front of its entrance. These were erected not only to guard the house and chase away evil, but also to serve as an artistic decoration. These stone lions are usually arranged according to a set of rules. Generally speaking, there should be a pair of them, a male and a female, with the male on the left and the female on the right (from the view of a person walking out of the gate). This conforms to the traditional Chinese philosophy of yin and yang, which has the precept of "male left, female right." As seen in this picture, the male lion, on the left as one exits the gateway, usually has an embroidered ball, while the female lion is often shown with a baby lion. Both lions squat on the Buddhist Mount Sumeru, covered with brocade. They look at each other with their heads cocked, displaying cheerfulness amid serenity and majesty.

This close-up of the eaves of a traditional Chinese building shows various types of auspicious animals. These decorative animals are generally called "ridge animals," and serve to both guard the house and bring luckiness. *Chiwen* (one of the sons of dragon) is ensconced on both ends of the ridge of the house, serving to repel disaster and fire. The lion is often featured on the roof. In addition to its heroism and intrepidness, as well as its protective and evil-dispelling qualities, the lion carries a wish for everything to go well, because "lion" is homophonous with "thing."

Detail of the crane roundel pattern

The backboard of this armchair features openwork decoration with cloud patterns that set off a crane roundel in the center. A rare bird in China, the red-crowned crane can fly very high with its call piercing the sky. In many Taoist stories, people that become immortals eventually change into cranes. Therefore, the crane is regarded as a divine bird among the Taoists. In addition, a crane can live 50 to 60 years, an extraordinary life span for a bird. Therefore, the crane is a symbol of longevity in China, giving the pattern on this chair the allegorical meaning of "the crane brings you a long life."

A butterfly in love with flowers often symbolizes a romantic and wonderful love story. The most famous classical story is the tragic "Romeo and Juliet" tale of Liang Shanbo and Zhu Yingtai, lovers unable to marry who eventually fly away in the form of a pair of butterflies in pursuit of a pure and genuine love. Thenceforward, the sight of a pair of butterflies would always remind people of this sad and touching story. The butterfly pair embroidered on the pillow flies to and fro gracefully in tandem, as harmonious and attractive as a pair of young people deeply in love.

This toilet case, marked by exquisite workmanship and valuable marble inlay, has a copper-clad hinge shaped like a beautiful butterfly. Always regarded by Chinese people as auspicious, the butterfly not only represents beauty and love, but also symbolizes fortune and longevity, because it is homophonous with "the aged." Since the butterfly has so many desirable allegorical meanings, it is no wonder that people like to use its image to express hopefulness and wishes for good fortune.

With the symmetrical shape of a butterfly, this copper handle attaches equal importance to practical function and aesthetic impact. As the butterfly is always associated with fresh flowers and spring, it symbolizes hope, desire, freedom and love, as well as longevity, because of its homophonous connotations (the word for "butterfly" sounds like that for "septuagenarian"). As it has so many auspicious connotations, its use on objects, even such a small handle as this, can bring pleasure and comfort to people using it every day.

The horse has not only been a friend of human beings since ancient times, but has also played an indispensable role in production, life and war. In the Tang dynasty (618 − 907AD), the horse symbolized the authority of a ruler. A horse often connotes "an instant success," meaning that one has done something so smoothly that success is achieved from the very beginning. People love horses, regarding their forms as the combination of power and beauty, and regarding their spirit as embodying loyalty and righteousness. Therefore, the horse appears often in traditional artworks. In the restaurant pictured here, the war-horse statue not only serves a practical purpose, partitioning the space between dining tables, but also provides a decorative touch with its ancient and elegant shape, evoking a nostalgic appeal.

The technique of high-relief has been used for this war-horse wall decoration along a walkway. With simple lines and realistic shapes, the posture and verve of this war-horse have been vividly demonstrated. Called "Telebiao," it is one of the six steeds in the "Zhao Mausoleum" of the Tang dynasty Emperor Taizong (also known as Li Shimin). All six of the stone-carved steeds have three-patterned manes and tied-up tails, typical of war-horses in the Tang dynasty. In addition, the saddle, stirrup and other accoutrements accurately represent the decoration of war-horses at that time. These "six steeds" were the most favorite war-horses of the Emperor, and helped him to achieve military pre-eminence during the process of establishing the Tang dynasty. Eventually, they died heroically on the battlefield, earning them limitless affection from their master for their loyalty. When the mausoleum was under construction, Emperor Taizong ordered their statues to be created so that they could accompany him in eternity.

Homophonous with "surplus," "fish" stands for affluence and abundance in traditional Chinese culture. "Lotus" is homophonous with "consecutive." Therefore, the pattern of lotus and fish on this teapot has the allegorical meaning, "There is a surplus for consecutive years," expressing the desire for a rich and peaceful life year after year.

The tablecloth and napkin seen here are embroidered with several lovely goldfish, which echo the fish pattern on the small cups in the distance. As a favorite ornamental fish in China, the goldfish has so gorgeous a color that it can be called a natural artwork. In ancient times, the raising of goldfish was usually an amusement of the rich and noble, so the goldfish carries loftier connotations than those of ordinary fish. In addition, as "goldfish" is homophonous with "gold and jade" in Chinese, it expresses a desire for wealth.

This apron panel board on the pedestal of a couch-bed is engraved with the pattern of sheep. As one of the earliest domesticated animals, the sheep has always been regarded as an auspicious animal by the Chinese, and is often used as decoration. As "sheep" is homophonous with "auspicious" in ancient Chinese, it stands for fortune and luckiness. A lamb kneeling down while suckling has long been regarded as a symbol of filial piety. Such traditional auspicious sayings as "three sheep can bring fortune" are also often evoked by the image of sheep. Even the origin of the Chinese characters for "beauty" and "kindness" has a close relationship with sheep. From these examples, we can see the varied positive qualities with which sheep have been linked over the centuries.

In ancient China, one of the most important functions of the screen wall was to mark status; it was generally placed behind the master or an important guest, to indicate special standing. The screen wall in the picture, in addition to partitioning the space, also has a desirable allegorical connotation due to its pattern of entwining peonies in a vase. This traditional type of lively flower pattern symbolizes good fortune and festivity. With its interweaving and continuous pattern, it carries the connotation, "multiplying endlessly." Various types of plants, including the lotus, peony and grape, can be used in entwining patterns, each shaded with different meanings. In this picture, entwining peonies invoke endless wealth and honor, while the vase symbolizes safety and peace. Together with the deep-red, antique-style wood-shelf that adds a note of festivity, they bring a feeling of classical elegance and auspiciousness to the entire space.

Chapter Two   Plants

Because of their graceful forms and gorgeous colors, flowers, grasses, trees and fruits have been popular among Chinese artists since ancient times, their images appearing in works ranging from painting to pottery to furniture. In addition, many carry auspicious connotations, which may related to the plant's shape or growth characteristics, to an auspicious word that is a homophone to its name in Chinese, or even to ancient legends in which it is featured. The allegorical meanings can roughly classified into categories: invoking wealth and rank, desiring longevity, looking forward to a harmonious family, and expressing aspirations.

Of the plants representing wealth and rank, the peony and gourd are among the most impressive. A decoration featuring the peony can bring an atmosphere of good fortune, wealth and honor to an ordinary and plain space, while a round and lovely gourd-shaped artwork can become an expressive, wordless supplication for prosperity.

The enduring vigor and greenness of the pine, and the many

The ornamental perforated window is a common architectural element in classical gardens. It can serve as a "frame" within a space, allowing people to enjoy the scenery glimpsed through it in the distance. In this picture, several slim bamboos appear framed by the hexagonal window, offering a tranquil and elegant sight. With its upright bearing, the bamboo symbolizes a modest and upward spirit. Because it resists coldness, remains evergreen and would rather break than bend, bamboo also connotes tenaciousness and intrepidness. Therefore, since ancient times, the bamboo has been an important symbol for Chinese scholars. A famous line of poetry states, "I would rather refrain from eating meat than live in a place with no bamboo." Because bamboo rises up quickly, section by section, it is widely popular among common folk as well. Therefore, the scene in this picture, with its bamboo grove outside, would be appreciated by people of any background.

legends about the peach, have led both to become representative of longevity. We can imagine what a climax a plate of peach-shaped birthday cakes can bring to a birthday party of an elderly person, and how much joy and comfort a screen carved with a picture of the pine can bring to those going about with their challenging daily life.

As both the grape and pomegranate are characterized by a large number of seeds, Chinese people, who attach special importance to the family, naturally regard them as auspicious, representing a large number of descendants. Therefore, when a wedding ceremony is held, a pomegranate will often be placed on the desk in the bridal chamber, with its skin peeled off, exposing its many seeds. A traditional Chinese canopy bed engraved with bunches of grapes is also regarded as an indispensible piece of furniture in the bridal chamber.

Known for their reserve, scholars in China have often used particular plants to subtly express their aspirations. In traditional artistic works, bamboo often represents a person's ambition and spirit, fragrant thoroughworts connote solitude and leisure, chrysanthemums symbolize aloofness and pride, and so on. In

In this scene, the designer has used a technique from classical gardens, "borrowing a scenic object." Here, the moon-cave window serves not only as a decoration, but also as a frame, "borrowing" the scene painted in the room beyond. This exquisite painting has at its center the peony, in all its richness and fullness, symbolizing wealth, rank and good fortune. In addition, the roundness of the picture echoes with the shape of the window. There is also an allegorical layer added—the peony and moon-cave window refer to traditional Chinese poetry featuring "beautiful flowers and full moon."

the rooms of these scholars, one may also find wood carved with plums, or an ink stone carved with lotus leaves, each of which carry their own connotations, showing the rich auspicious symbolism of plants.

In addition, auspicious patterns that combine different plants can be seen everywhere. The peony, *yulan* (magnolia) and Chinese flowering crabapple together can represent "wealth and rank in harmonious, prosperous families." Gourds and weeds together invoke "tens of thousands of generations of descendants." "Friendship between virtuous persons" is represented by the orchid and *lingzhi* fungus. And as a final, and extremely well-known, example, the pine, plum and bamboo are known as the "three friends of winter."

The wallpaper decorating this restaurant shows blossoming peonies from floor to ceiling. These gorgeous and bold flowers are worthy of their auspicious connotation of wealth and rank. What is extraordinary is that the painter has depicted them with a single color instead of many bright colors. The feeling of wealth and rank is conveyed with only the light gold ground color, thus displaying subtle taste. The wallpaper has a classical flavor and a strong decorative sense, setting off the modern furniture in the room.

This partition is carved throughout with gourds and their interwoven vines, providing lively decoration along with auspicious references. As "gourd" is homophonous with "fortune and prosperity," and it is closely related to immortality in Chinese mythologies and legends, it is seen an auspicious object, invoking luckiness and protection from evil and monsters. In addition, as a large number of small gourds branch off from the continuously stretching vine, it is often used to invoke the hope for the continuance of a line of descendants for tens of thousands of generations. The gourd has many traditional references, including "endless succession of descendants" and "tens of thousands of generations spanning a long time." Setting off the table setting's traditional colors of sapphire blue and bright yellow, this partition is a strong design element that also brings auspicious connotations to enhance this classical dining environment.

Because of its vitality, strength and permanent greenness, the pine enjoys the title of "the immortal tree," representing longevity in the eyes of Chinese people. Also because of its resistance to frost and snow and its ability to withstand the frigid winter, it is one of "three plant friends who thrive in cold winter," commonly known as "three friends of winter," together with the bamboo and plum. Its height and upright posture, as well as its grandeur and solemnity, make it a symbol for steadfastness and faithfulness. People admire these desirable connotations of the pine, and thus often use it as decoration in order to evoke these qualities. In this picture, the potted pines have not only brought a natural greenness to the dining space, but also a sense of refinement and allusion to tradition.

The porcelain bowl on this long and narrow table is decorated with lovely, ripe peaches, which symbolize longevity and good fortune. Patterns on Chinese porcelains usually take into consideration not only the beauty of the plant but also its intrinsic vital energy. Like traditional Chinese painting, porcelain decoration endeavors to capture a lively spirit. The goal of the artist here is not to create an absolute realistic rendering of peaches. Instead, the artist strives to depict an idealized peach, using abstraction and gorgeous colors to capture its essence.

Detail of the porcelain bowl

Lotus leaves stand upright and graceful above water. They wave gently and elegantly with a light breeze, and in a gale, offer a vigorous sight resembling waves. Therefore, the beauty of lotus leaves has been extolled in classical essays dating back to ancient times. In addition, the lotus is an important symbol in traditional Chinese culture as "lotus" is homophonous with "peace" and "harmony." When applied as a decorative element, the lotus can create an auspicious and serene environment.

A natural feeling is created in this room by distributing botanic landscapes here and there. In this lotus pond, the still surface of the water, the scattered pebbles and the gusts of fragrance from the flowers together offer a quiet and tranquil environment, adding a note of pure refreshment to the auspicious atmosphere invoked by the lotus. The designer has decorated the pond-bank with wood planks whose natural textures continue the fresh feeling of the landscape, and whose dark, straight lines echo the classical atmosphere of the decoration. In this scene, the "outdoor" landscape and the elegant indoor furniture are successfully combined into a graceful whole.

This cabinet combines the raised ends typical of Chinese furniture with a classic pattern of interwoven grapevines on the openwork side panels. Comprised of a large number of fruits in bunches, grapes symbolize a large number of descendants in a family, while the branches, leaves and vines are continuous and interwoven, representing permanence and prosperity. These desirable connotations are appealing to anyone looking forward to wealth, status, good fortune, peace and family happiness. The traditional-style cabinet here is set off by a large red couplet on the wall, giving the space a strong traditional Chinese flavor.

In traditional Chinese buildings, the support structure or bracket between the beam and the pillar is called a *queti*. Due to the pomegranate's large number of seeds, it is frequently used as an auspicious symbol invoking a wish for a large number of descendants. Together with the wood-engraved pattern of the bat above it, it means "more sons and greater fortune." In addition, as there is more than one pomegranate on this *queti*, and "pomegranate" is homophonous with "generation" in Chinese, there is another layer of auspicious meaning, "fortune for all generations."

The canopy bed is traditional among Han people, the ethnic majority in China. This canopy bed has three railed sides and an entrance screen, marked by an exquisite carving. Again, the pattern of grape, with its plentiful fruits and interwoven vines, is used here to symbolize the family's wish of a large number of descendants. A bed like this would often be part of a bride's dowry, providing a festive and auspicious touch. Over time, fewer and fewer people in China have come to use this kind of traditional furniture, and some have adapted it to other uses. As shown here, this canopy bed has instead become a unique setting where its owner can taste tea and meet friends. While its function may change, the bed's beauty and symbolism remain.

The subject of this decorative mural painting, the plum, is one of the traditional famous flowers in China. With its elegant shape and delicate flowers, the plum blossoms alone in the spring in advance of any other flower, even during snow and frost, giving it the name of "a messenger of spring." Countless artistic works extolling the plum have emerged over the centuries, dating back to ancient times. People regard it as representative of good fortune, elegance and fortitude. In this space, the unsophisticated posture of the plum also balances the resplendent and magnificent luxury of the space around it.

China is renowned for its porcelain production, and among its porcelains, blue-and-white porcelain can be called the king, with its status remaining unshakable for more than 700 years. While blue-and-white porcelain ordinarily features a white background, this type with a blue background and white flowers is also common. The plum pattern painted all over the body not only invokes spring and elegance, but because of the plum's five petals, also symbolizes the traditional "Five Fortunes" (longevity, affluence, good health, virtue and "natural death"). This porcelain, a true manifestation of key concepts of traditional Chinese culture, is set against Western-style candlesticks on the same table, adding interest to the space while embodying inclusiveness and diversification.

The orchid, attributed with a noble and pure character, is known as "the gentleman among flowers." It also stands for the pursuit of integrity and virtue. The idiomatic expression of "a solitary orchid blossoming in a quiet valley" connotes refinement and rising above the pursuit of wealth and fame. According to legend, as a divine plant, the orchid can foretell good or bad luck. If a room is haunted, the orchid in it will fade. The characteristics attributed to the orchid also have much in common with the Buddhist spirit. As one of the six offerings of Buddhism, the orchid can be also known as "a Buddhist friend" or "a Buddhist flower." People often use the orchid, as shown here, as an offering to the Buddha, bringing fragrance and tranquility to the room, and as well as a sense of peace and detachment to the mind.

The architectural structure in this picture, a tile end or eaves tile, is called a *wadang*. In traditional Chinese buildings, people often decorate the *wadang* with patterns that have desirable connotations, so as to bless their family members, protect their home and chase away evil. The type of *wadang* features the orchid, which, in addition to those qualities discussed earlier, is bestowed with such honorary titles as "the fragrant national flower" and "the flower with unmatched fragrance." It is uniquely blessed with four elegances (elegance in scent, color, style and spirit). In past centuries, people often referred to an elegant poem or essay as an "orchid-like work" and a good friend as an "orchid-like friend," thus giving an extremely high appraisal to the orchid. In addition, the orchid has long been respected and admired because of its resistance to cold and frost. Therefore, people have often chosen to feature the orchid on the *wadang*, not only because of its auspicious connotations, but also to encourage themselves or their descendants to aspire to the desirable qualities represented by the orchid.

In this interior space, the designer has created an unrestrained and natural "outdoor" environment, with bamboo playing the major part. On one side, lush bamboo is used to set off sections of a wall, interspersed with perforated windows and a pebble-covered track, giving the feel of a genuine classical garden. In contrast, on the other side, bamboo conceals and sets off the glass, thus blocking the modern street-scene beyond the window. In addition, indoor furniture with an ancient and natural style has been selected to continue the harmonious atmosphere of the room.

This brick wall sets off plants, such as bamboo and fragrant thoroughwort, and calligraphic scrolls. An elegant language of decoration underlies the design. As plants resisting frost, cold and snow while remaining evergreen, the bamboo and fragrant thoroughwort allegorically indicate superiority and elegance, and are greatly admired. In addition, they seem simple, detached and serene, and are thus reputed as "gentlemen." The two kinds of plants are often grown together, not only because they bring a connotation of "association between gentlemen," but also in order to complement the tranquility of the space.

The lotus has many traditional associations; it is one of the four auspicious flowers, one of the "Eight Treasures" and one of the "Nine Symbols" in Buddhism. Lotus is often used figuratively to refer to Buddhism. For example, the Buddhist world is also called "lotus world," the Buddhist scripture is also called "lotus scripture" and the Buddhist throne is also called "lotus throne" or "lotus platform." Due to its close associations with Buddhism, the lotus is seen to have a holy, tranquil and unsophisticated disposition. The statues in this picture have successfully conveyed this spirit with the help of simple and pure color and shape. In harmony with the decorative style of the environment around it, the lotus sculptures create an auspicious and peaceful atmosphere.

The golden doors of this food-preparation cabinet are decorated with branches of peonies and *yulan* flowers, full of classical glamour and spirit. The peony represents wealth and rank, while *yulan* is homophonous with "magnificent hall," a general term for palaces, fairy domiciles or luxury residences. These two kinds of flowers, which together connote "wealth and rank in harmonious and well-off families," create a feeling of resplendence, prosperity and nobility. While it has practical functions, this elegant food-preparation cabinet has a strong decorative character, and subtly sets off the vermilion that is the major color of the surrounding space.

The scene depicted on this decorative porcelain plate relates to the widely popular story of the Eight Taoist Immortals. According to legend, they were transformed from common people to immortals through excellent practice. They represent all kinds of people—male and female, young and old, rich and poor, noble and humble. Unlike other immortals, who may be viewed as remote and even sanctimonious, they are widely accessible and popular. There is also a belief that they represent personifications of the "Eight Diagrams" formerly used in divination, and the "Five Elements" (metal, wood, water, fire and earth). Of the many legends about them, the most famous is the legend of the "Eight Immortals crossing the sea." In this story, upon returning from appreciating flowers on the Penglai Divine Island, a fabled abode of immortals, they each use their respective magical instruments to cross the East China Sea, instead of taking a boat. From this story, we have the saying, "Like the Eight Immortals crossing the sea, each one shows his or her prowess." As these immortals are said to often do charitable deeds in the human world, they are extensively worshiped as auspicious symbols.

Chapter Three   Figures

The association of certain human figures with specific auspicious meanings may have originated with ancient "ghost and deity" cults and primitive religions. As auspicious symbols, these human figures can be roughly classified into such types as Buddhist and Taoist immortals, historical celebrities, and beautiful ladies and boys.

Images of immortals have persisted over centuries, with forms often becoming abstracted and stylized, making them easily recognizable. These include the Buddhist Arhats, the Eight Immortals of Taoism, the Door-god, and the Three Stars of Fortune, Prosperity and Longevity. Some have their origins in Buddhism, Taoism or Confucianism, while others come from folk mythologies and legends. With mysterious and supernatural powers, they can bring good or bad luck to people, as well as punish evil-doers or commend good deeds.

Statues of the God of Wealth enshrined on a table are widely popular, as are pictures of the Door-god, which are commonly

This carved panel features a central roundel with the God of Longevity standing under a pine accompanied by child with a divine peach in his hand, connoting congratulations on a birthday. The God of Longevity is usually pictured with a walking stick. This refers to an episode during the Han dynasty, when Emperor Mingdi invited all people over 70 years old to a banquet, bestowing each guest with an exquisitely-made walking stick. Those who carried the walking stick could then enjoy various privileges, popularizing the practice of showing respect to and remaining obedient to one's elders. As there was a carved culver, also known as a turtle dove, on the top of this walking stick, it was called a "culver stick." Over the ages, the walking stick in the hand of the God of Longevity has become one made of peach-wood. This association is especially appropriate as the wood is said to be able to eliminate illness, strengthen the body and prolong life, and the peach itself also symbolizes longevity.

pasted on the gate or front door when celebrating Lunar New Year. Ridge decorations on roofs or pattern decorations on gable walls often feature the figures of the Eight Immortals traveling across the sea, because people believe that these immortals can bring safety and protection from evil or monsters.

China, with its long history and rich culture, has a multitude of revered and much-told stories and legends. Many protagonists of these stories are well-known for their vivid personalities and outstanding deeds, and have become symbolic of specific qualities or characteristics. For example, the Seven Sages of the Bamboo Grove (Taoist scholars from the third century) can be seen to represent expressing oneself fearlessly in a self-possessed fashion. Lin Hejing, a famous poet who lived in seclusion "with the plum as his wife and crane his child," epitomizes a noble and upright life. Liang Shanbo and Zhu Yingtai, the "butterfly lovers" discussed in Chapter One, represent the pursuit of freedom and love. People use these figures in a variety of works to express admiration for the qualities they represent, as well to show their own aspirations.

Pictures of beautiful ladies often reflect the life of women in

Placed prominently in this restaurant, the pillar features a natural root-like carving with an auspicious picture of the "Three Stars." These divine beings have their origins in ancient cults that worshiped Nature and the sky, specifically Jupiter, the Big Dipper and the South Pole Star. The ancient people endowed these three with extraordinary divinity and unique personal charisma. Eventually, influenced by the imperial system and adopted by Taoism, the Three Stars became increasingly influential among the common people. They became the protagonists in various types of artistic works, from painting to poetry. In addition to the Three Stars, the pillar is engraved with other images symbolizing longevity and good fortune such as the pine, crane and white deer, adding to both the artistic and auspicious effect of the work.

the upper stratum of Chinese feudal society. Each dynasty has its own style and characteristics, but in a broad sense, these images represent beauty and harmony, as well as a serene and prosperous state of life. Therefore, many porcelains and frescoes feature these lovely women in elegant poses.

Images of healthy and charming boys are often seen in Lunar New Year paintings or on porcelains, carrying aspirations for a large number of descendants or wealth and good luck. Sometimes, a boy descends from the sky riding a kylin, which represents babies (in particular, sons) sent by a kylin. Boys with an upward-raised face and a finger pointing to a distant bat in the sky symbolize looking forward to the descent of fortune. A boy holding a carp in his arms represents the hope for a surplus of money every year. As we can see from these examples, many of the auspicious connotations of images of boys refer to a strong and large family or prosperity.

In China, there is a tradition at the Lunar New Year of pasting paintings on one's gate or door in order to chase away evil and protect the home. One popular picture is that of a Door-god, whether it is the Civilian Door-god, Military Door-god or Fortune-invoking Door-god. Over the dynasties, these Door-gods have varied, but the most widely accepted are Qin Qiong and Yuchi Gong, two generals from the Tang Dynasty revered for their skill in martial arts and ability to intimidate ghosts. People have come to believe that pictures of the two generals can dispel monsters and ensure the safety of their domiciles. Here, the designer integrates the folk custom of using Door-gods as decoration with the modern architectural structure, thus creating an interesting environment with classical connotations.

This is a statue of the God of Wealth, who is commonly enshrined in people's homes to invoke prosperity and status. The God of Wealth has various identities, which have developed and changed over time. One is Zhao Gongming (Marshal Zhao, God of Wealth), with a face as black as iron, a steel whip in his hand, and riding a black tiger. He became an immortal by cultivating himself according to the religious doctrine. Another is the God of Money and Silk (a Civilian God of Wealth), with a white face and long hair. He holds a treasure basin in his hand inscribed with the four Chinese characters of 招财进宝, meaning "invoking wealth and treasure." A third is Guan Yunchang (Marshal Zhao,God of Wealth), who is famous for keeping his promises and attaching importance to personal loyalty. In addition, there are other identities, such as the Wuxian God of Wealth, who is said to often rob the rich to help the poor and punish evil people to promote good deeds. The God of Wealth in this picture is relatively similar to the traditional image of the God of Money and Silk. Whatever the specific form, the God of Wealth's allegorical connotation of bestowing fortune and invoking wealth remains unchanged, as does the people's interest in and use of these images.

The painting hung near the dining table expresses its theme of "sending babies/sons" through layers of artistic symbolism. First, in the picture, a fairy accompanies the boy riding on a kylin to the human world, referring to the traditional belief of "fairies sending sons." Next, as the kylin itself also connotes "sending sons," the theme is reinforced. In addition, as the child holds a lotus flower in his hand, and "lotus" is homophonous with "consecutive" in Chinese, the picture expresses the wish to "give birth to one baby after another." The different components, in addition to creating a lively picture, form a strongly auspicious pattern.

In this space, functionality and quirky modernity have been interestingly incorporated with traditional Chinese-style elements that carry auspicious meanings. For example, the stone used as the pedestal of the dinner table looks ancient and unsophisticated, with a pattern of two celestial beings: He (written with the character 和, pronounced like "lotus" in Chinese) and He (written with the character 合, pronounced like "box")." During traditional wedding ceremonies, the scroll of the two celestial beings, He and He, would be often hung up, as "lotus" and "box" are homophonous with "harmony" and "uniting efforts," thus expressing a wish that the newly-weds live in conjugal bliss to a ripe old age. In addition, this wish is reinforced by the decoration of two divine boys, one holding a lotus flower in his hand, the other holding a round box, out of which fly five bats.

The figure shown on this ink stone sits against the plum as if somewhat intoxicated, accompanied by a crane. He is Lin Hejing, a famous poet in the Northern Song dynasty (960 – 1127AD) whose story has been much told over the centuries. He lived in seclusion at the foot of Gushan Mountain near the West Lake, Hangzhou. With no wife and children, he instead devoted himself to planting plums and raising cranes, eventually regarding the plum as his wife and cranes his children. Written at the peak of his poetic perfection, a couplet in one of his poems, "Dappled shadows hang aslant over clear shallow water; Secret fragrance wafts in the moonlit dusk" aroused a craze of extolling plums among the literati. Admired for his literary talent as well as his unrestrained spirit, people often use this quotation to represent a noble and upright life of reclusion.

This restaurant's interesting decorative partition uses an abstract pattern based on that of traditional shelves. Scattered along the partition at intervals are gold-painted carvings featuring scenes from the famous story, *The Romance of the West Chamber*. In this love story, Cui Yingying, the daughter of a prime minister, eventually became the wife of Zhang Junrui, a student from a poor family, after breaking through much resistance. As the representative work of Wang Shifu, a famous playwright in the Yuan dynasty (1279 – 1368), *The Romance of the West Chamber* spread far and wide, expressing discontentment with and resistance to the feudal system of marriage, as well as the yearning for and pursuit of the ideal of love. This design gives the space a charming and romantic feeling, enhanced by the vermilion of the sofas.

This full-length openwork screen not only has a functional component, dividing the space into relatively independent compartments, but also incorporates classical themes into the design. The gold patterning of the screen sets off porcelain pictures of various colors, depicting beautiful ladies. This kind of traditional picture chiefly reflects the life of women of the upper stratum in feudal society, symbolizing beauty with their lovely apparel, and harmony with their natural and graceful bearings. This type of picture also expresses an overall wish for a rich life.

The decoration on this wall is the famous *Scroll of Eighty-seven Immortals*. Although it is an anonymous work devoid of bright colors, it has been highly admired as one of the most classical religious paintings, and eulogized by such masters as Xu Beihong. With lines full of vitality, this scroll depicts eighty-seven immortals marching forward on the way to the court of the God of the Prime Origin. The exquisitely-drawn figures include the South Pole Lord of Heaven and the East Lord of Heaven, leading their boy and girl attendants, as well as other immortals. The scroll is harmonious with this classical and elegant interior, also giving it a feeling of spirit and divinity, as we can almost all feel the "divine gowns fluttering and the wall moving with the celestial wind."

Chinese people enjoy decorating their homes with porcelains, and vases of various colors can be seen most often. Vases not only have a beautiful shape and elegant patterns, but also symbolize peace and security because "vase" is homophonous with "peace," enhancing their popularity. One commonly-seen arrangement is the placement of a vase and a mirror on either end of a long and narrow table in the drawing room, together with a chime clock in the middle, connoting "lifelong peace." A pair of vases means "remaining peaceful and secure forever." In this picture, exquisite porcelains of various colors, placed with a picturesque irregularity, set off one another. This arrangement not only invokes peace and security, but also has an artistic flair.

Chapter Four   Objects

There are many objects that carry traditional auspicious meanings; some are homophonous with an auspicious word, and some are believed to chase away evil and invite good fortune. They not only include articles for daily use, implements for writing, and musical instruments, but also decorations and artworks with special allegorical connotations. Others are items from beyond the real world, including the magic implements used by immortals in ancient Chinese legends. Passed down through the generations, and often becoming abstracted, decoration using auspicious objects has become widely popular.

Objects may be pictured together, enhancing or altering their connotations. Meaning may often depend on objects being homophonous with lucky words or symbols, forming a sort of visual language. For example, a pen, a silver ingot, a *sheng* (a reed pipe wind instrument) and a hat together mean "one will certainly get promoted," while a pen and silver ingot together with a jade *ruyi* (an s-shaped wand or scepter) jointly connote "things will

The traditional *ruyi*, with the shape of a hand, has transformed over the ages to take many shapes: a roundel, a cirrus cloud, *lingzhi* fungus, and the Chinese character 心 (meaning "heart") among others. The *ruyi* in this picture is in the shape of *lingzhi*. Usually, large *ruyi* serve as a decorative furnishing, while small *ruyi* may be presented as a gift, to express an auspicious wish. By skillfully using the shape of the *ruyi*, this door handle combines a desirable allegorical connotation with its practical function. Made of dark wood, like that of the door, the *ruyi* handle heightens the classical and luxurious style of decoration.

certainly develop as one wishes."

For some objects, the image carries meaning that is directly related to the object's function. For example, the incense burner is used in prayer ritual, so as time has passed, the image of an incense burner in and of itself has come to represent something auspicious. In addition, in China, incense also signifies "there is no lack of successors," so an image of an incense burner carries the meaning, "successors emerging continuously."

Many musical instruments also have a desirable allegorical connotation. For example, the Eight Sounds (eight different ancient musical instruments made respectively of metal, stone, string, bamboo, gourd, clay, leather and wood) can jointly play out a piece of melodious, lively and pleasant music. Therefore, these instruments, including the bell and musical stone, can be seen as symbolizing festivity.

Writing implements have an important place in traditional Chinese culture, particularly in relation to the refined life of the literati. The "Four Treasures of the Study," i.e. the writing brush, ink stick, paper and ink stone, represent praise for and admiration of a scholar with profound knowledge and high cultural

This is a jade double dragon *ruyi*, whose name carries the allegorical connotation, "things go as one wishes." The *ruyi* in its earliest time had a practical function. The end of its handle had the shape of a finger; in short, it was a back scratcher. In the Ming dynasty (1368 – 1644) and Qing dynasty (1644 – 1911), its shape slowly transformed, morphing into this double dragon shape, among others. Its function also changed, as it became an auspicious object used exclusively for appreciation and enjoyment. At that time, *ruyi* made of various valuable materials were used as royal decorations or rewards to officials. Today, beautiful and elegant *ruyi* are still used in diplomacy as national gifts.

attainment.

There are many other objects that serve as auspicious symbols. Such articles as a *fangsheng* (a lozenge made with a red or peach-colored rope in ancient China), ancient coins, rhinoceros horn, etc., are all called auspicious treasures.

Under the category of decorative or art objects with lucky connotations, we find the "Five Kinds of Auspiciousness," which are five jade ritual utensils, including the *bi* (a round flat piece of jade with a hole in it), *huang* (a semi-circular jade pendant), *gui* (an elongated pointed tablet of jade held by ancient rulers on ceremonial occasions), *cong* (a rectangular jade with round holes) and *zhang* (a kind of jade tablet shaped like half of a *gui*).

Looking to legend, we find the "Covert Eight Immortals," which refer to the magical implements of the Eight Immortals. These include the gourd of Li Tieguai, the lotus flower of He Xiangu and the sword of Lü Dongbin. The so-called "Eight Auspicious Articles of Buddhism," including the magic conch shell, magic wheel and treasure umbrella, also fall into this category. As spiritual, divine and magical articles, they are often used by people with the hope of chasing away evil and invoking

This study is decorated with antique flavor. The set of patterns carved meticulously on the cabinet includes an incense burner, a vase, a *ruyi* and a fly whisk. As seen earlier, the incense burner is an indispensible part of religious ritual, giving it divine and supernatural associations. Its use for the endless burning of incense gives the object another layer of allegorical connotation, meaning "there is no lack of descendants for a family." "Bottle" is homophonous with "peace" in Chinese, while the fly whisk, an article carried by Taoist and Buddhist immortals, is believed to have supernatural power, chasing away evil. These objects were selected to decorate the cabinet not only because they have auspicious connotations but also because they demonstrate the owner's appreciation of Chinese tradition.

good fortune.

In traditional buildings, some of these objects appear as decoration carved on a beam or *fang* (the square wood connecting two pillars). Some are depicted on the door of a cabinet, while others are applied in the shapes of ornamental perforated windows in gardens. The objects themselves may be designed as artworks to decorate an interior. Regardless of the form or location, they always express wishes for good fortune.

This decorative partition's vase shape, a shape often used for doorways in classical gardens, provides visual interest while allegorically signifying good fortune (due to the connotations of homophones of the word for "vase," discussed earlier). The designer has achieved a remarkable balance among the colors as well between straightness and curve, and emptiness and solidity. As a final touch, a vase of flowers sits in the partition's hollow, thus enabling the "vase" to be worthy of its name.

In classical gardens, doorways in different shapes, such as this one, can often be found. This doorway is shaped like a gourd, which is homophonous with "fortune and prosperity." It is also believed to bring luck; with a small neck and big belly, it is easy for an object to enter and difficult to leave. So, the gourd is regarded as an object that can absorb wealth. In addition, as the object carried by Li Tieguai, one of the Eight Immortals, the gourd also implies "delivering all living beings from worldly sufferings." In a picturesque garden with lush flowers and trees, this gourd-shaped doorway appears as another natural element, harmonious with its surroundings.

The engraving of 福, invoking happiness or fortune, has broken the uniformity of this patterned window, forming an exquisite focal point. The rounded and exuberant brushstroke used for the character 福, as well as the pattern of entwining branches around it, contrasts with the simple horizontal and vertical lines of the rest of the window, making this most important part stand out, vividly highlighting the auspicious theme.

Chapter Five   Symbols

Traditional auspicious patterns include not only real and legendary animals, plants, figures and objects, but also abstract symbols that have desirable allegorical connotations. These signs can be roughly classified into those that invoke the traditional "Five Fortunes," those that represent wishes for status and honor, and those that reflect elegance purity and aspiration. These abstract symbols are widely popular and often quite festive, leading to their extensive application not only on their own but also as part of a decorative pattern. Various symbols with different allegorical connotations may also be brought together in a pattern that has its own particular meaning.

As noted in the Preface, the so-called "Five Fortunes" refer to longevity, affluence, good health, virtue and "natural death." Therefore, the related symbols include the Chinese character 寿, symbolizing longevity; the Chinese character 囍 connoting festivity; ancient coins (often interlinked to represent wealth); and the Chinese character 福, invoking happiness or fortune. In many

This close-up of a roof shows laced drip tiles decorated with a pattern of the Chinese character 寿. Meaning "longevity," this character reflects a wish for health and long life, an especially universal desire. Perhaps it is because of this that the character 寿 can be written in hundreds of forms, adapting easily to coordinate with various designs. The use of 寿 in the decoration of residences represents the desire for peace and health for all the family members within.

domestic dwellings, we may see a large 福 engraved on the screen wall, or a pattern incorporating 寿 on a decorative screen.

A desire to bring status and honor to one's family is a widespread yearning. Dragon patterns, formerly limited in use to royalty, have come to represent nobility and esteem. Patterns of floating clouds against an azure sky symbolize a fairyland or elevated status. Over the years, these signs, which were originally seen in imperial architecture and design, have been increasingly used in decoration of domestic dwellings and furniture.

With their beautiful shapes and elegant symbolism, "ice crack" patterns with a bamboo leaf shape invoke naturalness and elegance, as do various patterns of flowers and grasses. These forms are often applied in the decorative perforated windows of classical gardens, on furniture in scholarly studies, and areas closely integrated with nature, providing a touch of elegance and refinement to the decoration.

Patterns using the symbol 回 or the endless knot serve to express continuity and endurance. Often used as the border for floors, ceilings or partitions, they can also be used in artwork or with other objects to reinforce the auspicious tone. For example,

Incorporating traditional elements into an otherwise modern style has become an important trend in contemporary design. For example, the door handles make use of the symmetry of this stylized 寿 pattern, carrying traditional cultural references, while the simple lines and color scheme have a modern feel. The contemporary red sofas and light fixtures within the space, with their festive colors, also echo the auspicious connotation of the door handles.

a stele with the 寿 (longevity) pattern encircled by many patterns will further reinforce the original allegorical connotation of congratulations on a birthday, forming a pattern representing wishes for a long life.

Originally meaning that two happy things occur at the same time, 囍 (double happiness) is now usually used for weddings, expressing the happiness of a husband and wife in love with each other. Pasting up a red paper symbol during a wedding ceremony is a Chinese custom. In addition, just as shown in this picture, people also use this character to decorate related articles; here, the red candle necessary for a traditional wedding ceremony was turned, by a skillful design, into a candlestick featuring a hollowed-out "double happiness" pattern. The photo frame shows another example of the variety of this character, using a geometric and abstracted form for the mirror frame.

Although these blue-and-white porcelain jars patterned with 囍 are not particularly valuable or famous, their simple form and strong native flavor are interesting and attractive. These jars are commonly displayed on long and narrow benches. Here, on the central axle of this room, they are arranged in a row, conveying a strong sense of order. Their classic simplicity contrasts with the pageantry of the Western-style chair located nearby, while their cyanine color contrasts with the scarlet of the chair. These interesting contrasts bring a new sense of life to traditional Chinese style.

With the increasing popularity of Chinese style, bars and other Western settings are increasingly being decorated with traditional Chinese elements, often updated with a modern twist. For example, the sides of this bar counter are lined with glazed bricks featuring ancient coins at their center. The gorgeous glazes, together with the wealth-invoking symbolism represented by the ancient coins, imbues this space with an atmosphere of wealth and luxury. In addition, the classical shape and rose-red color of the melon-shaped lights used for the pedestals of the bar stools enhance the Chinese-style charm and magnificence.

This is a traditional-style chair with a comb-shaped back. Among all chairs in classical styles, the chair with a comb-shaped back is the most natural and elegant due to its simple lines and unadorned shape. This classical simplicity is echoed in the room's lattice window and wood table. Even in the details of the chair, the use of the double coin pattern is understated, subtly invoking wealth, and reminding one of the leisurely, affluent and noble lives of immortals.

Because of its upward turned ends, this table is called a "raised head table" or "long table with up-turned ends." Tables like this are often used to admire scrolls of painting and calligraphy. Here the table is used as an altar, with a golden Buddha ensconced on it. This table's decoration prominently features the *ruyi* cloud head pattern. Originally used in Buddhist ritual, the *ruyi* later evolved into an object used exclusively for appreciation and enjoyment. Therefore, in addition to the auspicious connotations of regular cloud patterns, the *ruyi* cloud pattern also has a relationship to Buddhism.

The backs of the armchairs in this picture are decorated with a carved *ruyi* cloud head pattern. These special cloud patterns are rolled and turned into the shape of *ruyi*, the S-shaped ornamental object that now serves as a symbol of good luck. Here, the auspicious connotations of the clouds are enhanced by the Buddhist references of the *ruyi*. Indeed, in this room, which is arranged according to the traditional principle of symmetry, the *ruyi* pattern is opposite the sublime figure of the Buddha.

The gold decoration on the door lintel is called the meandering dragon or formalized dragon pattern. This pattern often consists of the dragon head together with dynamic geometric lines. Sometimes, the pattern is further abstracted, with only the crisscrossing and zigzagging geometric lines, and no dragon head at all. The dragon pattern here, like other dragon images, symbolizes dignity and fortune, while "meandering" is homophonous with "descendant" in Chinese, so this pattern has a further auspicious connotation. The gold color of the meandering dragon pattern highlights its magnificence, adding to the impact and elegance of the space.

This wood beam is carved with water patterns, the beautiful lines forming rolling and unfolding waves. According to a legend, when a flood dragon emerges from the water, surging swells appear in the background. Water and wave patterns have come to have many allegorical meanings, often representing good fortune and respectability. In ancient times, generals would wear "wave and cliff" patterns on their embroidered robes. Sea water invokes the tide, which is homophonous with "(imperial) court" in Chinese, so water patterns became decorations exclusive to official gowns, and served to identify officials and government ministers.

Often a small but crucial detail, which originally seems insignificant, serves to unify the space's theme and endow it with meaning—this is the so-called "finishing touch." In the decoration of this walkway, the finishing touch is the hollowed 回 pattern that serves as the *queti* (bolster) between wood beam pillars. Although small in size, it subtly points out the classical Chinese style of decoration, tying together the carpet patterns and the color scheme.

The 回 pattern, a geometric pattern evolving from the thunder pattern found on potteries and bronzes, invokes luckiness and profundity. As this pattern winds along without end, it is commonly referred to as "endless wealth and rank." It is an interesting pattern, regular and uniform and yet capable of various changes. The 回 pattern occurs widely, from wood carving to porcelains to architectural decorations, and is mostly used as a border decoration or background pattern. However, as shown in this screen, it can also appear as the feature decoration, adding an ancient, elegant and auspicious note to the space.

In this picture, the wall is decorated with partitions often seen in traditional buildings, generally consisting of a panel with openwork carving together with a solid skirting board (the lower part of a partition door). In this picture, the carved panel is decorated with a pattern representing longevity, derived from the symbol 卍, which in Sanskrit means a lucky or auspicious object. As a magical incantation in ancient times, the 卍 pattern was often used on amulets or as a religious symbol, often representing the sun or fire. As shown in this picture, this pattern stretches outward in all directions, and can be used in many variations. A widely-used auspicious symbol, this kind of chained pattern naturally lends itself to such meanings as "continuous and endless" and "endless happiness and longevity."

In this space, a black screened partition not only serves as background, but it is also an important decorative component by itself. These beautiful carved 卍 patterns together have an auspicious connotation, referring to the symbol's original appearance on the bosom of the Buddha, connoting luckiness, fortune and longevity. In addition, the texture and lightness of the carving contrasts with the heavy and solid stone pedestals, while the blackness of the wood contrasts with the grayness of the stone. Modernity and classicism, solemnity and vivacity have been intermingled in the space, bringing balance and harmony.

In this corner of a study, the simple and elegant furniture goes well with the ornamental perforated window behind. The window has an ice crack pattern in a bamboo leaf shape has an auspicious connotation since the bamboo can symbolize safety, peace, loftiness and uprightness. This pattern has a natural, classical and elegant appeal, so it is quite appropriate to use in the decoration of a study, where it also brings a touch of the outdoors to an indoor space.

The ice crack pattern in a bamboo leaf shape has been used to decorate this floor lamp, giving it an elegant and auspicious feeling, without affecting the function of illumination. This decorative pattern is often seen in the architectural decorations of gardens, where it invokes the classical Chinese romantic sentiments of "the shadows of flowers move with the moonlight," and "a winding path leads to a secluded spot." In this picture, the lamp, together with the furniture and decoration in the traditional style around it, gives the entire space a classical Chinese charm.

In classical Chinese gardens, doorways are often given the shape of flowers and grass, so as to express a philosophy of close integration between the man-made and nature. This generous and elegant doorway in the shape of crabapple is a prime example. Although in nature, crabapples don't necessarily have four petals, in the design of traditional porcelains, furniture, etc., crabapples are usually depicted with four petals. This distinguishes them from plum patterns, which typically have five petals, and also served to add a reference to the saying, "as smooth as four seasons."

Small paths in gardens are often paved with pebbles of different colors in various patterns that highlight the spring scenery. The pattern in this picture is charming, resembling crabapples, with their lingering fragrance, fallen along a path. The blossoming crabapples appear to form a brocade, giving a feeling of festivity, wealth and rank.

This wood partition is marked by a simple and elegant flower pattern. Due to the four petals, it represents the crabapple. Delicate, gorgeous and bewitching, the crabapple has many associations, including the "national flower," "the fairy among flowers" and "a flower that can understand the words of people." In addition, as "crabapple" is homophonous with "hall (family)" in Chinese, the crabapple often appears—together with other flowers, grass and objects connoting fortune—in auspicious patterns symbolizing "wealth and rank in harmonious and well-off families" and "five generations of a family living under the same roof." This kind of refined and beautiful pattern complements the style of the other decorative elements in the room, giving the entire space a feeling of elegance and simplicity.

The "language of decoration" of this conference room is straightforward and terse, using simple shapes along with symbols that are easily recognizable to a Chinese audience. The patterned openwork panel manifests this approach. Here, the pattern of the meandering dragon has been shaped into a stylized 寿 roundel in the center. A close look reveals four flying bats at the edges of the roundel, with one in the center, which is a well-known auspicious pattern. In addition, four vases with flowers surround the roundel, forming what is commonly known as the "archaic pattern." Therefore, this panel expresses many desirable allegorical meanings including fortune, longevity, dignity and knowledge.

This washstand features exquisite carving along with designs that carry profound allegorical connotations, giving it artistic value and cultural meaning. The zigzagging and crisscrossing pattern of the meandering dragon has been adopted as the decoration of the chair back. The overall regularity and geometry of this pattern is interspersed with rounded and delicate cloud patterns. The cloud head has the shape of a *ruyi*, bringing its own elegance and auspiciousness to the washstand. The meandering dragon and the cloud pattern both symbolize dignity, honorability and good luck. Their appearance together here emphasizes these symbolic meanings.

The lamp box is cleverly designed; its orange-yellow light illuminates the room while emphasizing the carved patterns, giving the whole interior an elegant and classical touch. The use of the phoenix pattern invokes festivity and fortune, while the crabapple (with its four leaves formed by cloud patterns) symbolizes nobility and elegance. Similar patterns have also been adopted as the decoration on the cushions of the seats and chairs, bringing harmony to the overall decorative effect.

Many kinds of auspicious signs have been used in the decoration of this elevator hall. A golden 回 pattern and a plant meandering pattern have been respectively adopted for the beams and *fangs* (square wood connecting two pillars) near the ceiling. The endlessly meandering pattern of auspicious flowers and grass also symbolizes desirability and permanence. The floor features a mosaic with an ice crack pattern in a bamboo leaf shape, giving the space an elegant and even scholarly disposition. Although beautiful, these patterns are not merely decorative—together they implicitly express the desire for elegance, wealth, dignity and the continuance of numerous generations.

Chapter Six   Synthesis

In addition to each of the categories discussed in previous chapters, auspicious patterns may be created through combination. Synthesis combines two or more things, separated by type, period or background, and these combinations result in their own specific auspicious connotations.

"Phoenix flying through peonies" is one typical example of how this combination can work. This common picture combines the peony, blossoming in nature, with the phoenix, a divine bird in legend. The symbolism of wealth and auspice represented by each is magnified by their combination, constituting a more festive and auspicious picture.

Similar pictures include those that bring an animal and a plant together. Some examples popular in China include: an aigrette and a lotus flower, symbolizing in a homophonous way a wish for success for the candidates for the imperial examination; or an official figure stroking a deer, a homophone for a wish for a promotion and a raise of salary. Other combinations bring

A delightful and vivid pattern is carved on this gourd-shaped perforated window. Several small squirrels frolic in a leisurely and carefree way amid grapevines, feasting on the grapes. This is a traditional picture that connotes a large number of descendants through several allegorical references. First, as the grape has bunches of fruits, it represent many descendants. In addition, "squirrel" corresponds with "zi" (meaning descendant) in the twelve Earthly Branches, a Chinese system for reckoning time, and the squirrel is good at producing babies. The gourd shape of the window adds another layer of meaning, as "gourd" is homophonous with "fortune and prosperity." So these various symbols come together to express the wish for endless descendants, fortune and wealth.

together objects with animals or plants. Many of these examples are traditional pictures often seen in architectural structures and interior decoration.

There are also many combinations of concrete objects and abstract signs. One well-known example is the flying dragon with an auspicious cloud pattern, often seen on a *huabiao*, an ornamental column. On the embroidered squares of official gowns (rank badges), the combination of auspicious animals, including the crane, sparrow, lion and tiger, set off by patterns of seawater, was often seen.

The most frequently-seen synthesis of animals and symbols is the pattern of five flying bats (homophonous with "fortune") encircling a roundel with the character 寿 (longevity) in the center. This pattern demonstrates the wish to gain both fortune and longevity. Its lively composition and the flexibility inherent in its pattern have lead to its extensive application in various types of traditional design.

In addition, different patterns may be combined within a design, even if that combination does not produce a new allegorical meaning. The various symbols, each contributing its individual

This Master armchair, a type of old-fashioned wooden chair, features stylized dragon patterns on its back, and its head support and backboard are carved with bats and auspicious clouds. Specifically, five bats hover among the clouds, symbolizing the "Five Fortunes descending from the sky," longevity, affluence, good health, virtue and "natural death." Chinese people attach special importance to benevolence, kindness and generosity, because they believe virtue is the cause and root of fortune, which, in turn, is the outcome and demonstration of virtue. Only a virtuous person can achieve the other fortunes. As to the fifth fortune, ancient people hoped to be able to know the date of their death in advance, and to leave the human world peacefully and comfortably, without any unexpected disaster, painful illness, worries or a troubled mind.

desirable connotation, may still enhance the decoration and the overall auspicious atmosphere. One example is the roof decoration of traditional buildings. The roof may include *chiwen* (one of the sons of the dragon) on the ridge, the character for longevity on the drip tiles, and a dragon roundel on the gable. While together these do not create a specific meaning, the integration of various types of auspicious patterns serves to reinforce the owner's wish for an advantageous, secure and happy life.

In this wall decoration, behind lotus flowers, a magpie perches on water weeds. As a messenger of good news in Chinese culture, the magpie often represents luck in artistic works. As "lotus" is homophonous with "consecutively" in Chinese, the combination of these two articles carries a traditional auspicious meaning of "achieving success consecutively in imperial examinations." What sets this wall decoration apart from other traditional patterns of this kind is the technique of bas-relief and the use only of white, instead of the customary representation in thick ink and strong color. This adds a note of elegance and purity to the festivity of the theme.

The stately Master chair and floor lamp make this more of an indoor landscape than a quiet area for rest. The openwork pattern on the chair's backrest is a kylin treading on auspicious clouds and looking back at the sun, representing peace and good fortune. In contrast, the upper roundel features a carving of clouds and a dragon. This corresponds with the decorations of the lamp, where a divine dragon darts amid auspicious clouds, emerging now and then, vividly expressing its celestial spirit, and of course symbolizing a lofty and dignified status at the same time. The coordination of these decorative elements serves to clearly and thoroughly convey auspicious meaning.

Left: Detail of the lamp holder

Right: Detail of the backrest of the chair

This floor-to-ceiling openwork wood screen borrows design techniques from classical gardens. By portraying a vase-shaped doorway, which is common in gardens, the screen adds the wish for peace and safety symbolized by vases to the auspicious connotation of longevity conveyed by the carving of the pine and crane. The red-crowned crane is not only a rare bird but also a symbol of longevity. Since the pine resists cold and always remains green, it is regarded as a symbol of remaining young forever in spite of having been weather-beaten for many years. The combination of all of these elements highlights a wish of congratulations on a birthday, together representing peace, safety and longevity.

Although originally used as a kind of outdoor furniture in gardens, the drum-shaped stool made of pottery or porcelain is now also used in modern indoor design. This is because of its beautiful shape and pattern, as well as the auspicious meaning it contains. With butterflies dancing among entwining peonies, the lively pattern shows beautiful spring scenery while expressing an allegorical theme of "happy reunion." In addition, the gorgeous dark-red background color is vivid and festive.

In this design of this space, classical Chinese simplicity and the sumptuousness of Western style are both employed, creating a contrast that remains curiously balanced. Especially eye-catching is the fact that the Western-style sofa is upholstered with a pattern of "phoenix flying through peony flowers," which is often seen in rural areas in China. Its bold coloration, exaggerated shapes and smooth lines give it vibrancy and festivity. This intensity dialogues with the low-key simplicity and plainness of the wooden cabinets and tables, as well as the gracefulness of the Western style footstools, filling the entire space with an intriguing appeal.

The open medallion decorating this scroll leg table is unique: the hollow area is bordered on inside by a *ruyi*-shaped auspicious cloud and on the outside by a peach-shaped pattern. In this design, a double auspicious connotation is expressed with a smooth and simple form. Due to a legend about a divine peach, the Chinese regard the peach as a symbol of longevity, and together with the God of Longevity and the crane, it expresses birthday congratulations in many traditional pictures. The *ruyi*-shaped auspicious cloud connotes both good fortune and luck. Therefore, the pattern consisting of both the peach and the *ruyi* auspicious cloud represents a multi-layered wish for longevity, fortune and continuous good luck.

As seen in this detail of a partition board door, the patterned panel is carved with auspicious flowers and grasses alternately inserted within the pattern of meandering dragons, symbolizing wealth, rank and honor. On the other hand, the waist of the skirting board is engraved with a pattern of "mixed treasures," including such auspicious utensils as the vase and incense burner, symbolizing peace, safety, luck, festivity, and abundant descendants. Together with the auspicious cloud patterns on the hardware and the flowers behind the door pulls, the door's decorative program expresses people's wishes for fortune in various aspects of their life.

The articles in this picture were must-haves in the 1970s and 1980s for a wedding ceremony in Shanghai or many other parts of China. They are typical of design trends of that time. Take, for example, this red vacuum flask. Using modern realism to depict roses and peonies, it represents a happy life and enduring love. It follows tradition in expressing festivity with the double happiness symbol. Overall, the design, combining ancient and modern, as well as Chinese and Western elements, shows an early example of "mix and match" design, which remains prevalent at present.

This pendant lamp has a simple and modern shape, but its color and pattern follow ancient traditions. With a pattern composed of dark-red peony blossoms interspersed with outlined auspicious clouds, it forms a sort of scroll with the celestial scene of "peonies blossoming amid clouds." It captures the nobility of the peony and the good fortune invoked by the clouds. While abstract, this design concretely represents people's desire for nobility and good fortune. It successfully adds a traditional charm and a lively auspicious feeling to the more slick and modern interior.

This antique washstand remains in use, having been updated with the modern function of the faucet but retaining its classical elegance. On this elaborately engraved washstand, there are many beautiful decorative patterns that capture the viewer's attention. The central subject is that of bats flying out of a round box held by the two celestial beings, He and He, connoting "fortune shines on harmony and unification" in a homophonous way. Around this decoration, there are auspicious flowers and grasses, meandering dragons and double carp patterns, each of which invokes good fortune and festivity.

Detail showing the central subject

Just like the animals and plants depicted on ancient rock paintings, the patterns on this cushion are marked by a bold and unrestrained beauty, reminding one of ancient animal totems or cults. As the king of all animals, the tiger has the power to dispel evil. The deer, a divine animal, is homophonous with "prosperity" in Chinese, and also symbolizes the prospect of promotion for officials. The flowers and birds encircling them not only add to the naturalism of the scene, but also symbolize desirability and vitality in a vivid form. In addition, the green of the fabric sets a strong contrast to the red around it, making a harmonious yet distinctive whole.

This wall decoration's outer frame features carved butterfly patterns on the four corners and double coin patterns on the left and right sides. The butterfly allegorically connotes longevity, auspiciousness and a desirable love, while the double coin symbolizes endless wealth and rank. The meandering patterns of dragons and flowers covering the central carving represent dignity, nobility and fortune. The designer has brought these two carved pieces together, making a cohesive decoration with abundant allegorical meaning. The exquisite style of the wall decoration and the naturalness of the background wall of fir form an interesting contrast. This is really a decorative highlight in the space.

This stone carving shows a vase holding flowers and an incense burner placed on an incense table. As the incense burner allegorically connotes a large number of descendants because of its endless burning of incense, and "vase" is homophonous with "peace" in Chinese, the combination of these two articles represents a wish for endless peace and safety. In addition, the vase and incense burner are not only objects used in daily life but also two of the auspicious utensils known as the ancient "mixed treasures."

The ornamental perforated windows in classical Chinese gardens are exquisite and unique. They provide decoration while also serving as a unique frame for the scenery beyond the window. Through this window, we can see a section of whitewashed wall setting off several emerald bamboos, appearing pure and graceful. With a pattern of abstract butterflies and flowers, this perforated window is poetic and picturesque, representing the theme of "a butterfly in love with a flower." The window adds liveliness and color to the flickering bamboo shadows beyond the window.

The stone carving on this wall is divided into two parts, which are brought together by symmetrical composition, similar themes and related allegorical connotations. The panel on the left contains cranes and bamboo branches. As the crane represents longevity and "bamboo" is homophonous with "congratulation," this combination represents "congratulations on a birthday." On the right, the magpies on plum blossoms allegorically connote "radiant with joy" in a homophonous way. Therefore, these panels together invoke longevity, auspiciousness and happiness.

This sumptuous carpet adds a warm and welcoming note, while its crane pattern echoes the traditional furniture and decoration, creating an atmosphere of auspiciousness and festivity to the entire space. The round traditional pattern consisting of the crane, the Chinese character for longevity, the peach and auspicious cloud is called the "crane roundel." The carpet is covered by a pattern of auspicious clouds and the crane. Set off by the clouds, the flying crane appears more immortal and otherworldly, thus highlighting its Taoist identity as a divine bird and emphasizing good fortune as the theme of the pattern.

A view of the carpet from another angle

In classical Chinese gardens, footpaths decorated with patterns made from gravel are seen quite often. In this picture, the small path is fully covered with crabapple patterns. Even in frigid winter, when almost all flowers have faded away, this path will provide spring-like scenery. The butterflies interspersed among the flowers not only add liveliness to the pattern, but also create a beautiful scene of butterflies dancing gracefully in the sea of flowers. This picture expresses people's love of spring, when all things flourish, and further symbolizes their yearning for an advantageous life.

As mentioned previously, the crane is known as an immortal bird in China. The tortoise is a well-known symbol of longevity in many countries including China, Japan and the Republic of Korea. Therefore, this bronze crane with a *lingzhi* fungus in its mouth, standing on the back of a stone tortoise, represents a traditional art work expressing congratulations on a person's birthday. Such a statue is often seen in ancient Chinese palaces, expressing the wish for good health and long life by combining two animals representing longevity together with the *lingzhi* fungus that can prolong life. There is another layer of meaning—the tortoise is male and the crane is female, connoting eternal love.

With a unique shape, this chess table looks like a drum-shaped stool often seen in classical Chinese gardens. The patterns carved on the drum body are exquisite. The two scenes visible here indicate that the drum's pictorial scheme represents the saying, "Forever love (loving to an old age) is like a never-ending spring." This expresses the wish for every couple to respect each other and live a life as desirable as spring throughout their days. This type of auspicious pattern often includes an albatross (representing old age due to its gray head) and fresh flowers of the four seasons.

In this detail of a piece of furniture in a traditional style, we can clearly see a decorative pattern of a bat, which is homophonous with "fortune" in Chinese. This bat unfolds its wings in an inverted position, as if descending from the sky, connoting "fortune descending from the sky." The dragon pattern around it represents dignity, honor and peace, and the picture of "frolicking boys" drawn above it carries an auspicious atmosphere of conviviality and festivity. These decorative patterns together add a rich and auspicious tone to the entire piece of furniture.

Detail of the pattern of "a magpie on plum blossoms"

This round-backed armchair is decorated as if made from bamboo stalks, and its backboard is engraved with the auspicious pattern of "a magpie on plum blossoms." Plum, a flower that blossoms against frost and brings the first tiding of spring, is certainly enhanced by the lively magpie, invoking auspice and good news, chirping on a branch. Furthermore, "plum" is homophonous with "eyebrow" in Chinese; at the sight of a magpie on a branch of plum, people would often expect a lucky thing to occur to their family, causing them hope that "raises the tip of their eyebrows." No wonder this is an especially popular pattern in traditional style.

Detail view of the gate

The decoration of this gate is elegant and classical. On its lower part, the openwork chain patterns symbolize continuous wealth and rank. On the doorknob, a plate of pomegranates and litchis has been carved. The pomegranate is deeply loved because it is an auspicious plant symbolizing a large number of descendants, with its well-known allegorical connotation, "a pomegranate contains hundreds of seeds (a pomegranate brings along a hundred sons)." On the other hand, "litchi" is homophonous with "benefit," representing the desire of people for wealth. Thus, the decoration integrates wishes for wealth and family, delighting people coming and going through the gate.

Since the Qing dynasty, the decoration of Chinese buildings has become more and more complex, and its details have been increasingly abundant. Even beams and *fangs* are decorated with carvings, as shown in this picture. Here, a formalized dragon design sets off the flower basket and sword in the center. The sword of Lü Dongbin and the flower basket of Lan Caihe are two of the "Covert Eight Immortals," the magic instruments of the Eight Immortals. The sword can overwhelm monsters and the flower basket can communicate with all kinds of deities; the combination of all these patterns allegorically connotes "extolling and wishing for longevity." The carving in this picture is not only auspicious and lovely, but also is an integral part of the overall sumptuous design, which features meticulous workmanship and dazzling color.

In the pavement of Chinese gardens, mosaics or bas-relief decorations often appear at intervals to avoid monotony and enrich the artistic atmosphere. These decorations usually contain some auspicious patterns. This picture features a stone carving of a "pines and cranes roundel." As the pine is known as the "ever-young tree," and the crane is renowned as a celestial and divine bird, the combination of these two animals allegorically connotes long life and permanent youth.

Each of the skirting boards of this partition door combines auspicious patterns of plants and animals. With "a magpie on plum blossoms" as the theme, some of panels depict the scene of a magpie twittering and gamboling on the branches of blossoming plums, expressing joy for the advent of spring. With the theme discussed earlier of "forever love (loving to an old age) is like a never-ending spring," some of these patterns feature a Chinese rose blossoming in all four seasons (representing a permanent spring) with an albatross (representing old age). The waistline decoration of the skirting board adds to the auspicious atmosphere with its decoration of a "fresh flower enclosed in an archaic pattern."